AMITABHA BUDDHA

THOUSAND-HANDED GUAN YIN

BODHISATTVA IMAGE

VENERABLE MASTER HUA

# GREAT COMPASSION MANTRA VERSES

# GREAT COMPASSION MANTRA VERSES

Composed by
the Venerable Master Hua

English translation by the
Buddhist Text Translation Society

Burlingame, CA: Buddhist Text Translation Society

*Great Compassion Mantra Verses*

Published and translated by:
**Buddhist Text Translation Society**
1777 Murchison Drive, Burlingame, CA 94010-4504

©1999    **Buddhist Text Translation Society**
         **Dharma Realm Buddhist University**
         **Dharma Realm Buddhist Association**

Printed in Malaysia

First Chinese edition published 1982, Buddhist Text Translation Society, as
宣化上人偈讚錄 *(xuan hua shang ren ji zan lu)*

**First English edition**   2000
07 06 05 04 03 02 01 00    10 9 8 7 6 5 4 3 2 1


**Library of Congress Cataloging-in-Publication Data**

Tripitaka. Sutrapitaka. Mahakarunikacittadharani. English. Selections
    Great compassion mantra verses / composed by the Venerable Master
Hua; English translation by the Buddhist Text Translation Society.
    p. cm.
    ISBN 0-88139-518-8
    I. Title. II. Hsuan Hua, 1908- III. Buddhist Text Translation Society.

BQ1670.M353 E5 2000
294.3'85 21--dc21                                    99-044522

Note: Yale is used for the romanization of mantra syllables.

# Contents

# The Eight Guidelines of The Buddhist Text Translation Society

1.  A volunteer must free him/herself from the motives of personal fame and profit.

2.  A volunteer must cultivate a respectful and sincere attitude free from arrogance and conceit.

3.  A volunteer must refrain from aggrandizing his/her work and denigrating that of others.

4.  A volunteer must not establish him/herself as the standard of correctness and suppress the work of others with his or her fault-finding.

5.  A volunteer must take the Buddha-mind as his/her own mind.

6.  A volunteer must use the wisdom of Dharma-Selecting Vision to determine true principles.

7.  A volunteer must request Virtuous Elders in the ten directions to certify his/her translations.

8.  A volunteer must endeavor to propagate the teachings by printing Sutras, Shastra texts, and Vinaya texts when the translations are certified as being correct.

# Great Compassion Mantra

1. na mwo he la da nwo dwo la ye ye

2. na mwo e li ye

3. pwo lu jye di shau bwo la ye

4. pu ti sa two pe ye

5. mwo he sa two pe ye

6. mwo he jya lu ni jya ye

7. nan

8. sa pan la fa ye

9. swo da nwo da sye

10. na mwo syi ji li two yi meng e li ye

11. pe lu ji di shr fwo la leng two pe

12. na mwo nwo la jin chr

13. syi li mwo he pan dwo sa mye

14. sa pe e two dou shu peng

15. e shr yun

16. sa pe sa dwo na mwo pe sa dwo

    na mwo pe chye

17. mwo fa te dou

18. da jr two

19. nan e pe lu syi

20. lu jya di

21. jya la di

22. yi syi li

23. mwo he pu ti sa two

24. sa pe sa pe

25. mwo la mwo la

26. mwo syi mwo syi li two yun

27. jyu lu jyu lu jye meng

28. du lu du lu fa she ye di

29. mwo he fa she ye di

30. two la two la

31. di li ni

32. shr fwo la ye

33. je la je la

34. mwo mwo fa mwo la

35. mu di li

36. yi syi yi syi

37. shr nwo shr nwo

38. e la shen fwo la she li

39. fa sha fa shen

40. fwo la she ye

41. hu lu hu lu mwo la

42. hu lu hu lu syi li

43. swo la swo la

44. syi li syi li

45. su lu su lu

46. pu ti ye pu ti ye

47. pu two ye pu two ye

48. mi di li ye

49. nwo la jin chr

50. di li shai ni nwo

51. pe ye mwo nwo

52. swo pe he

53. syi two ye

54. swo pe he

55. mwo he syi two ye

56. swo pe he

57. syi two yu yi

58. shr pan la ye

59. swo pe he

60. nwo la jin chr

61. swo pe he

62. mwo la nwo la

63. swo pe he

64. syi lu seng e mu chywe ye

65. swo pe he

66. swo pe mwo he e syi two ye

67. swo pe he

68. je ji la e syi two ye

69. swo pe he

70. bwo two mwo jye syi two ye

71. swo pe he

72. nwo la jin chr pan chye la ye

73. swo pe he

74. mwo pe li sheng jye la ye

75. swo pe he

76. na mwo he la da nwo dwo la ye ye

77. na mwo e li ye

78. pwo lu ji di

79. shau pan la ye

80. swo pe he

81. nan syi dyan du

82. man dwo la

83. ba two ye

84. swo pe he

Guan Yin Bodhisattva

# Verses on the
# Eighty-Four Transformations of the
# Great Compassion Mantra

**1. na mwo he la da nwo dwo la ye ye**

With a kind, compassionate regard, a regard full of joy and giving,
He rescues all beings, transforming great-thousand world systems.
Gathering in those with and without prior affinities,
He helps them to end suffering, find joy, and return to the source.

## 2. na mwo e li ye

Our body, mouth and mind form a wheel that is this mighty dharani.
As the many-petaled lotus blossom just begins to open,
White, green, red, and purple light shines on us all.
Disciples of the Buddha have affinities to join the sages? celebrations.

### 3. pwo lu jye di shau bwo la ye

Holding a bowl, Contemplating Sounds saves us mortals;
Prescribing medicine to cure our ills, he nurtures the three thousand worlds.
Bowing in homage, we earnestly entreat him to answer our calls.
In various ways he fulfills all our heart' s desires.

### 4. pu ti sa two pe ye

Enlightening sentient beings plants causes for sagehood.
When we reach the unconditioned Way, we tally with the true mind.
As we benefit others and ourselves, our merit becomes perfected.
Thus, together we enter the *prajna* doors to liberation.

**5. mwo he sa two pe ye**

The wonderful functions of the lariat reach beyond words and thought.
Holding this, Bodhisattvas rescue those lost in confusion.
Chanting this mantra while contemplating brings samadhi.
To reach Buddhahood in this life is not impossible.

**6. mwo he jya lu ni jya ye**

The Great Knight Horse Whinny transforms the Saha world.
Relieving suffering, bestowing bliss, he cures our illnesses.
The dead come back to life when he gives them his sweet dew.
The Vajra Hand is too hot for vampires and demons to handle.

### 7. nan

Swallow the void and the Dharma Realm in a single gulp.
Our own tranquil nature is not inside or outside.
So it is! So it is! The causes are just like this:
Beginningless, endless, neither ancient nor modern.

## 8. sa pan la fa ye

The Four Kings who protect our world patrol night and day.
Rewarding good and punishing evil, they tame all demons.
Bodhisattvas appear by transformation to quell hordes of monsters.
Dragons coil and tigers crouch before the Dharma Lord.

16

### 9. swo da nwo da sye

The heavenly generals and troops exhibit matchless courage
That regularly turns the celestial demons into trembling cowards.
By changing faults and becoming good, the poor can get rich.
Attaining rebirth in Ultimate Bliss, we separate from suffering.

## 10. na mwo syi ji li two yi meng e li ye

Responses to requests are often amazing and hard to describe.
Due to the strength of samadhi, no prayer is left unanswered.
The Venerable Dragon Tree calms the demons' wrath.
Those who practice are free of disasters and attain Bodhi.

**11. pe lu ji di shr fwo la leng two pe**

Nishyanda Buddha, the fine and perfect reward body,
Protects and supports those who practice with the greatest mastery and ease.
Hearing their sounds, he saves beings of worlds in the ten directions,
So they leave mundane defilements—such is the might of the Dharma!

**12. na mwo nwo la jin chr**

Clear, pure Dharma-body Vairochana Buddha
Rescues vast numbers of beings here in the Saha world.
Developing Vajra-like rock-solid tough physiques,
We can climb up onto the other shore and reach *paramita*.

### 13. syi li mwo he pan dwo sa mye

Kindness makes others happy, compassion alleviates suffering.
By teaching multitudes of beings, we become Buddhas and Patriarchs.
This sheep-headed spirit king protects those who practice,
Keeping at bay tigers, wolves, and other beasts.

**14. sa pe e two dou shu peng**

The sweet dew anointing our crowns makes us feel cool and refreshed,
Saving countless beings who attain health and safety.
Those born in four ways in the six paths attain benefit and bliss.
Kindness, compassion, joy, and giving aid the Dharma King.

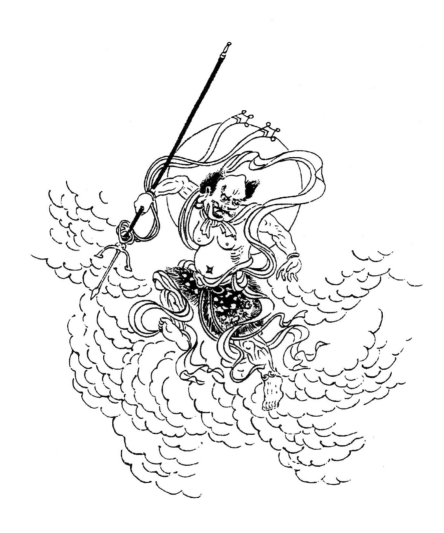

## 15. e shr yun

This yaksha deva king is wrapped in a tiger hide.
In rewarding good and punishing evil, he is dangerous and swift.
While patrolling in all four directions, he notes our merits and errors.
Maintaining justice, he makes sure that we each get treated equally.

**16. sa pe sa dwo na mwo pe sa dwo na mwo pe chye**

Contemplator of Sounds appears in the guise of a spirit king.
In his thousand hands, these Dharma jewels are an endless wonder.
A snake coiled round his crown and his black face tame monsters.
The Proper Dharma abides due to vows that are vast and deep.

## 17. mwo fa te dou

This line makes good people happy and evil people afraid.
Those worried and in suffering become far removed from sickness.
The Buddha Eye regards the entire Dharma Realm.
The golden wheel rolls over and destroys each and every demon.

## 18. da jr two

A vast and long tongue fills the three thousand lands,
While Contemplating Sounds appears to teach women and men.
All Arhats are worthy of offerings and killers of thieves,
And by benefiting self and others, enlightenment and practice are perfected.

**19. nan e pe lu syi**

Ghosts and spirits respectfully listen to these pure sounds.
Three eyes can see right into beings' hearts.
Our vows will be fulfilled and all we seek will surely be attained.
The myriad practices all lead us to enter the doors to prajna.

## 20. lu jya di

The lord of the Brahma Heaven commands spirit troops.
Bodhisattvas of ten directions each display a body
To rescue and liberate beings so they leave the sea of suffering.
Swiftly ascending the other shore, we find the city of tranquillity.

## 21. jya la di

This black spirit ruler assumes an awesome air.
North, south, east, and west—he can roam wherever he pleases.
Shocking the deaf, arousing the blind, this compassionate Lord
Never rests day or night in his rescue of beings.

## 22. yi syi li

Massive spirit troops in the Thirty-three Heavens
Revere and obey the commands of these secret efficacious phrases.
Rewarding good and punishing evil, they protect the proper teaching.
Throughout the world, peace and equanimity reign supreme.

### 23. mwo he pu ti sa two

With a firm, true mind we will gain a response to our seeking.
No request, no matter how great, will go unanswered.
Kindness and compassion brought to paramita rescues creatures.
When demons are subdued the Proper Dharma flourishes unhindered.

## 24. sa pe sa pe

Accumulated Fragrance Bodhisattva is an awesome and mighty spirit.
Ghosts of blue, yellow, red, white, and black hue
Toil and slave, obeying the teaching and changing themselves.
When responses mesh with the Way, all kinds of beings are saved.

**25. mwo la mwo la**

Urge each other on and share your vigorous resolve.
Join together in practice to perpetuate the mind seal.
Then when fruition of complete Bodhi enlightenment is yours,
You can rejoice among the Dharma Flower Assembly.

### 26. mwo syi mwo syi li two yun

Responding to those who are ready, he appears in boundless bodies.
With awesome spirit, he reveals things great and small, provisional and real.
This vajra indestructible body is forever free and at ease.
As his heavenly eye contemplates, his heavenly ear listens.

### 27. jyu lu jyu lu jye meng

My body and mind are empty, the world is empty too.
A mighty celestial general leads his celestial troops.
Patrolling in many lands, they investigate good and evil as they roam,
Rewarding merit, punishing transgressions precisely with no mistake.

## 28. du lu du lu fa she ye di

This fierce, heroic peacock shocks the mountain sprites.
Bodhisattvas issue commands as they patrol the entire universe.
Protecting the good, dispelling evil, and clearing up confusions,
This ruthless army exhibits its matchless courage in battle.

## 29. mwo he fa she ye di

Wherever there is great pain or great joy, there will be great compassion.
Cultivate wholesome Dharmas with a strength that knows no fear.
The jeweled pestle quells demons and protects practitioners
While also warding off the three disasters and eight difficulties.

### 30. two la two la

Appearing as a most unusual rare and mighty hero,
His adorned classic features are free of any flaws.
Using virtue to move people, his mind remains humble and sincere.
He is stern in appearance, yet gentle in nature.

## 31. di li ni

Troops led by a lion king verify our chants and incantations,
That number from thousands to tens of thousands to infinite times.
Amassing goodness through beneficial deeds, our merit is made full
And we achieve Bodhisattvahood, reaching levels of supreme fruition.

## 32. shr fwo la ye

Quelling all demons so the Proper Dharma can flourish forever,
A jagged bolt of lightning terrifies ghosts and spirits.
The universe clears and is pure as vampires' auras subside.
With the wisdom sun shining on high we rejoice in peace.

**33. je la je la**

Such fierce glaring scowls cause the deviant demons to cringe!
Such boundless awesome virtue protects every Buddha!
Beings one and all attain both peace and happiness.
When Bodhisattvas' deeds are done they laugh, "Ho! Ho!"

## 34. mwo mwo fa mwo la

Repressing cults and demons with displays of awesome spirit,
His great compassion saves the world; he is a King of Dharma.
With magnanimous equality he rescues us, expansively perfecting paramitas.
Beings with and without affinities attain *gate*.

## 35. mu di li

When not a single thought arises, the esoteric is penetrated.
With the aid of samadhi, the brilliant light of wisdom is revealed.
Buddhas all laud and praise good men and good women who
Close their eyes, clear their minds, and chant these true words.

### 36. yi syi yi syi

The mighty god Maheshvara is bold, yet often cruel.
Rewarding good and punishing evil, his merit is outstanding.
He enables the masses sunk in confusion to climb upon the far shore.
There is no beginning or end to the creatures he benefits and transforms.

## 37. shr nwo shr nwo

Appearing to be good, appearing to be evil, he gathers in all beings.
Now complying, now defying, he subdues our natures.
Returning to the source involves curing our own faults.
That way, our maha prajna wisdom gets brighter by day and by night.

### 38. e la shen fwo la she li

The Forty-two Hands are wonderful beyond scope or measure.
Penetrating heaven and earth, they aid and assist the confused.
Swift is their spiritual prowess with shields, bows, and arrows.
Bullies are tamed and the gentle get a chance to thrive.

## 39. fa sha fa shen

How majestic and courageous, yet kind and compassionate is this great general
Who subdues and tames us beings so we can leave the paths of confusion.
We should change what's bad, follow what's good, and perfect our practice
By developing blessings and wisdom and awakening to True Suchness.

**40. fwo la she ye**

Contemplating Sounds' teacher is the Host, Amitabha Buddha,
Whose forty-eight vows transform the Saha world.
Ultimate Bliss is reached through nine kinds of rebirth on three levels.
The Mahayana is expressed in the flowing water and blowing wind.

## 41. hu lu hu lu mwo la

Contemplating Sounds appears as a king of ghosts and spirits
Who forces the demons to submit and follow the rules and regulations.
Each and every being relies on the teaching and instructions.
The strong are pacified, and the weak are able to flourish.

## 42. hu lu hu lu syi li

This four-armed deity reveals an awesome spirit.
When the deviant demons observe that impressive magnificent air,
They take refuge with the Triple Jewel and start contemplating self-mastery.
Amassing merit and practicing good, they foster their virtue.

**43. swo la swo la**

Wholesome and clever expedients save those in the Saha world.
A display of five turbidities transforms hordes of demons.
Constant selfless practice will bring *paramita*.
Renouncing attachment to dharmas as well is the Mahayana.

**44. syi li syi li**

The wisdom that contemplates and the states that are contemplated
Are perfectly fused and at ease in the Nature of True Suchness.
Boundless resolve and vows benefit all living beings.
How inconceivable to be able to always reside in deep samadhi!

## 45. su lu su lu

When the many creatures speak the Dharma, who listens?
Worldly beings are formed by the solidifying of false thoughts.
The original source of the Buddhas is beyond the spoken and written word.
"Thus I have heard" is the function of great compassion.

**46. pu ti ye pu ti ye**

Using kindness, compassion, joy, and giving, the four infinite minds,
She reveals wholesome aspects to transform the untaught masses.
Gathering in beings, she helps them ascend to the other shore.
Returning her light she shines it within and goes back home.

**47. pu two ye pu two ye**

Contemplating Sounds may show up in an ugly evil shape
To restrain these stubborn and violent ones until they change their minds.
When prajna wisdom is revealed, everyone certifies to nonproduction
And enters again the Saha world to rescue sentient ones.

**48. mi di li ye**

Kindly displaying a compassionate air, he transforms evil people
Who feel so secure that even in dreams their spirit is clear.
The reward of blessings they attain is infinite and boundless as well.
Bodhi *prajna* arises from our own profound practice.

## 49. nwo la jin chr

Contemplating Sounds shows up as Venerable Dragon Tree,
Who, gathering those who are ready, helps them leave the firey pit.
Finding our way to the source is realizing proper enlightenment.
The Sutra of the Dharma Realm is unveiled from within a mote of dust.

## 50. di li shai ni nwo

Wearing a necklace of human skulls, he chants this mantra.
Wielding an iron spear, he makes his rounds day and night.
He awakens beings to do every kind of good deed
And not to fall into the boundless sea of suffering.

**51. pe ye mwo nwo**

The vajra pestle challenges the massive hordes of demons.
Using lotus blossom recitation beads, be mindful of Amitabha Buddha.
The thundering sound startles awake the dull and confused.
Coming out of the dream, we find even one word to be too much.

## 52. swo pe he

Wondrous auspiciousness dispels disasters and increases blessings.
The Buddha, Dharma, and Sangha Jewels emit brilliant light.
Singlemindedly reflect and practice bowing that transcends appearances.
Great Bodhi is what teaches and transforms beings everywhere.

### 53. syi two ye

How exquisite are his hallmarks and supremely subtle physical aspects!
How thoroughly he fathomed and entered every Dharma door!
He saves those with affinities, assuring them rebirth in Ultimate Bliss.
The Land of Stillness and Light is the truth within the true.

## 54. swo pe he

Bodhisattvas many as grains of sand in the Ganges River,
Poised atop a sea tortoise, chuckle, "Ho! Ho!"
The abundant ocean of Dharma rescues absolutely everyone.
All beings and I leave self and others behind.

**55. mwo he syi two ye**

When the massive bright light he emits shines on the whole world,
Those born from wombs, eggs, transformations, or moisture
    no longer hang upside down.
Beings in nine realms achieve Proper Enlightenment.
How lofty Eternity, Bliss, True Self, and Purity are!

### 56. swo pe he

He is foremost in spiritual powers, as well as transformations and changes.
Truly rare is his golden staff which saves those in the world.
Beings in the hells all receive this rare kindness, and
Are freed of obstacles and difficulties, resolving their minds on Bodhi.

### 57. syi two yu yi

According with their kinds, he appears as various gods to rescue them.
By joining in their work, doing good deeds, he attracts those with conditions.
Ignoring himself for the sake of others, he is truly selfless.
He vows that all beings will become worthy sages.

## 58. shr pan la ye

This time around the Bodhisattva appears as a goddess,
Bestowing the teaching for those who are ready and guiding the confused.
With gradual, gentle, and wholesome enticements, she instructs tirelessly.
Her kindness and compassion are fair and equal in gathering in beings.

## 59. swo pe he

Dispelling disasters and difficulties, purging demons of sickness—
The wonderful functions of the Jeweled Bowl are quite inexpressible.
Fulfilling every wish we have, he bestows fearlessness.
*Gate, gate, swo pe he.*

**60. nwo la jin chr**

With manifestations as many as a sea of dust motes,
   he appears in infinite bodies.
He diligently plows the field of the six perfections and the myriad practices.
Turning from the Small and embracing the Great is the Bodhi fruit.
Saving ourselves and teaching others is the *prajna* mind.

## 61. swo pe he

Planting causes and reaping effects, one nurtures good roots.
Ending birth and casting off death must be done by ourselves.
Work with courageous vigor to perfect the *paramitas*.
The practice of the Maha Enlightened Way is remarkably deep.

## 62. mwo la nwo la

The Jeweled Seal Hand and Eye of this great Bodhisattva
And the golden ax shatter the root of ignorance.
All afflictions of sentient beings are completely cut off.
A delicate lotus wells forth from the ground.

## 63. swo pe he

He roams at ease, and his spiritual powers transform the universe.
Clad in straw sandals, he strides atop the waves. How boundless his Dharma!
His sound, like the ocean's roar, awakens us from dreams and confusion.
Cowards muster their will; the greedy become incorruptible.

### 64. syi lu seng e mu chywe ye

Transforming and appearing as the Great Bodhisattva Medicine King,
He expels disease and eradicates plagues, saving millions.
Enabling beings to escape pestilence and leave suffering,
His sweet dew is sprinkled on the sprouts of those with feeling and awareness.

### 65. swo pe he

Through contemplative practice cultivation arises: homage to the Buddhas.
Blessings and wisdom make our Way-place adorned and magnificent.
If we can certify to deep profound prajna, then certainly
We can cross beyond all suffering, awakening to the eternal truth.

### 66. swo pe mwo he e syi two ye

Always complying with beings, he teaches those in the Saha land,
And the evil world of five turbidities, transforming demons.
Panning for gold in the sand, he searches ardently for sages,
Never wearying of trying to catch the moon in the water.

## 67. swo pe he

With the wordless true Sutra hanging ever by his side,
His wisdom matches the ocean; his samadhi, a lofty mountain.
When precepts and virtue are perfected, clear light shines everywhere.
Gathering beings in when they're ready, he saves those with affinities.

## 68. je ji la e syi two ye

His physical body in samadhi, he appears throughout the universe.
Seeing his form, hearing his name, frees us from the hells.
Fathoming life's one great matter, we have made it across.
Thus all of us are personally gathered in by the Enlightened King.

### 69. swo pe he

Cultivators of the Way, do not cheat yourselves.
It won't work to plug your ears while stealing a bell.
Barren blossoms cannot bear real fruit.
What a shame to let precious time pass by in vain!

**70. bwo two mwo jye syi two ye**

Having nothing to do, Bodhisattvas go looking for some work.
As they sit on exquisite lotuses, their brilliant light radiates.
Bestowing predictions of full enlightenment on all beings,
They perfect Nirvana that is certified to be without residue.

## 71. swo pe he

Heavenly goddesses scatter flowers as offerings to practioners.
Our precepts and Vinaya held strictly, our spiritual powers superb--
If we can then turn our light around and contemplate with ease,
Before long we will tally with the Great Awakening of Honored Ones.

## 72. nwo la jin chr pan chye la ye

His body unhindered, the great appears within the small.
His scope pervades north, south, east, and west.
The three-thousand system of worlds is but a single thought.
In no way can you, I, and others be separate from the mind.

### 73. swo pe he

When bowing and making offerings be earnest and sincere.
Incense, flowers, lamps, and fruit should be fresh daily.
Cultivation using the true mind is apart from any marks.
Making the three aspects of giving empty, we leave confusion.

**74. mwo pe li sheng jye la ye**

A thousand hands, a thousand eyes as well as great compassion
Change the whole world and brings us back across.
Kings among the heavenly demons accept this teaching.
Turn from evil, become good, and so quickly return.

**75. swo pe he**

Bowing without having bowed; practice with no concept of practice.
Realizing even emptiness is empty, what is there to seek?
Seeing through it all and putting it down is true freedom.
Roaming throughout the Dharma Realm we can do as we please.

**76. na mwo he la da nwo dwo la ye ye**

With True Emptiness as his substance and illusory form as his function,
He contemplates those in the world and saves them from sickness.
The responses that happen are timely and hard to imagine.
We blind and dull ones should certainly take refuge.

**77. na mwo e li ye**

Transforming and appearing as Universal Worthy who pervades all worlds—
He is seated in full lotus and ready with boundless Dharmas.
His hundred-jeweled, wheeled palm smashes the hells.
Amitabha Buddha is the Venerable Host of the Western Paradise.

## 78. pwo lu ji di

The eldest disciple of the Dharma King is the Venerable Manjushri.
Kindhearted, he transforms and teaches inhabitants of the Saha world.
With identical vows, they certify to infinite wisdom.
The Land of Stillness and Light is the village of ten thousand Buddhas.

## 79. shau pan la ye

Laozi said, "Five colors blind the eyes."
Contemplating Sounds freed his eyes and awakened to the Truth.
Upon a golden lotus he radiates rays of light.
Our original face does not come from our worldly family or ancestors.

## 80. swo pe he

Silk and earth, bamboo and hide, wood, stone and metal
Make eight notes that combine into endless scores of music.
Freeing his ear organ, he heard his own nature.
Even heavenly melodies wafting through space will not move his mind.

## 81. nan syi dyan du

Receiving, upholding, reading, and reciting these miraculous phrases,
Bestow blessings, be mindful and protective of everyone who practices.
Appearing in each world of the three thousand system,
Contemplating Sounds' nose freed itself of defiling smells.

**82. man dwo la**

Hold mantras and recite Sutras with a single mind.
When responses mesh with the Way, dirt can turn to gold.
Bodhisattvas' compassion: like the moon shimmering in water;
Living beings' awakening: freedom from the tongue and flavors.

**83. ba two ye**

This is a place beyond any place in space and the Dharma Realm
That contains seas of lands in number like motes of dust.
Those with and without affinities will all be taught and saved.
Those who believe, accept, honor, and practice are saints and sages.

**84. swo pe he**

This, then, is called the Great Compassion Dharani,
And, with the Forty-two Hands, is extremely rare in the world.
Only those with massive good roots encounter these.
What a shame it will be if we fail to cultivate this Dharma!

# Verse of Transference

May the merit and virtue accrued from this work

Adorn the Buddhas' Pure Lands,

Repaying four kinds of kindness above

And aiding those suffering in the paths below.

May those who see and hear of this

All bring forth the resolve for Bodhi

And, when this retribution body is over,

Be born together in the Land of Ultimate Bliss.

**Namo Dharma Protector Wei Tou Bodhisattva**

# The Dharma Realm Buddhist Association

The Dharma Realm Buddhist Association (DRBA) was founded by the Venerable Master Hsuan Hua in the United States of America in 1959 to bring the genuine teachings of the Buddha to the entire world. Its goals are to propagate the Proper Dharma, to translate the Mahayana Buddhist scriptures into the world's languages and to promote ethical education. The members of the association guide themselves with six ideals established by the Venerable Master which are: no fighting, no greed, no seeking, no selfishness, no pursuing personal advantage, and no lying. They hold in mind the credo:

*Freezing, we do not scheme.*
*Starving, we do not beg.*
*Dying of poverty, we ask for nothing.*
*According with conditions, we do not change.*
*Not changing, we accord with conditions.*
*We adhere firmly to our three great principles.*
*We renounce our lives to do the Buddha's work*
*We take responsibility in molding our own destinies.*
*We rectify our lives to fulfill our role as members of the Sangha.*
*Encountering specific matters, we understand the principles.*
*Understanding the principles, we apply them in specific matters.*
*We carry on the single pulse of the patriarchs' mind-transmission.*

During the following decades, international Buddhist communities such as Gold Mountain Monastery, the City of Ten Thousand Buddhas, the City of the Dharma Realm and various other branch facilities were founded. All these operate under the guidance of the Venerable Master and through the auspices of the Dharma Realm Buddhist Association. Following the Buddhas' guidelines, the Sangha members in these monastic facilities maintain the practices of taking only one meal a day and of always wearing their precept sashes. Reciting the Buddha's name, studying the teachings, and practicing meditation, they dwell together in harmony and personally put into practice the Buddha's teachings.

Reflecting Master Hua's emphasis on translation and education, the Association also sponsors an International Translation Institute, vocational training programs for the sangha and the laity, Dharma Realm Buddhist University, and elementary and secondary schools.

The Way-places of this Association are open to sincere individuals of all races, religions, and nationalities. Anyone willing to put forth his or her best effort in nurturing humaneness, righteousness, merit and virtue in order to understand the mind and see the nature is welcome to join in the study and practice.

# Venerable Master Hsuan Hua

The Venerable Master Hsuan Hua was also known as An Tse and To Lun. The name Hsuan Hua was bestowed upon him after he received the transmission of the Wei Yang Lineage of the Chan School from Venerable Elder Hsu Yun. He left the home life at the age of nineteen. After the death of his mother, he lived in a tiny thatched hut by her grave-side for three years, as an act of filial respect. During that time, he practiced meditation and studied the Buddha's teachings. Among his many practices were eating only once a day at midday and never lying down to sleep.

In 1948 the Master arrived in Hong Kong, where he founded the Buddhist Lecture Hall and other monasteries. In 1962 he brought the Proper Dharma to America and the West, where he lectured extensively on the major works of the Mahayana Buddhist canon and established the Dharma Realm Buddhist Association, as well as the City of Ten Thousand Buddhas, the International Translation Institute, various other monastic facilities, Dharma Realm Buddhist University, Developing Virtue Secondary School, Instilling Goodness Elementary school, the vocational Sangha and Laity Training Programs, and other education centers.

The Master passed into stillness on June 7, 1995, in Los Angeles, California, USA, causing many people throughout the world to mourn the sudden setting of the sun of wisdom. Although he has passed on, his lofty example will always be remembered. Throughout his life he worked selflessly and vigorously to benefit the people of the world and all living beings. His wisdom and compassion inspired many to correct their faults and lead wholesome lives.

Here we include the Records of the Mendicant of Chang Bai written by the Venerable Master to serve as a model for all of us to emulate.

*The Mendicant of Chang Bai was simple and honest in nature.*
*He was always quick to help people and benefit others.*
*Forgetting himself for the sake of the Dharma,*
*    he was willing to sacrifice his life.*
*Bestowing medicines according to people's illnesses,*
*    he offered his own marrow and skin.*
*His vow was to unite in substance with millions of beings.*
*His practice exhausted empty space as he gathered in the myriad potentials,*
*Without regard for past, future, or present;*
*With no distinctions of north, south, east, or west.*

**Dharma Realm Buddhist Association**
**The City of Ten Thousand Buddhas**
2001 Talmage Road, Talmage, CA 95481-0217 U.S.A.
Tel: (707) 462-0939   Fax: (707) 462-0949

**The International Translation Institute**
1777 Murchison Drive
Burlingame, CA 94010-4504 U.S.A.
Tel: (650) 692-5912  Fax: (650) 692-5056

**Institute for World Religions (Berkeley Buddhist Monastery)**
2304 McKinley Avenue
Berkeley, CA 94703 U.S.A.
Tel: (510) 848-3440  Fax: (510) 548-4551

**Gold Mountain Monastery**
800 Sacramento Street
San Francisco, CA 94108 U.S.A.
Tel: (415) 421-6117  Fax: (415) 788-6001

**Gold Sage Monastery**
11455 Clayton Road
San Jose, CA 95127 U.S.A.
Tel: (408) 923-7243  Fax: (408) 923-1064

**The City of the Dharma Realm**
1029 West Capitol Ave.
West Sacramento, CA 95691 U.S.A.
Tel: (916) 374-8268

**Gold Wheel Monastery**
235 N. Avenue 58
Los Angeles, CA 90042 U.S.A.
Tel: (323) 258-6668

**Long Beach Monastery**
3361 East Ocean Boulevard
Long Beach, CA 90803 U.S.A.
Tel: (562) 438-8902

**Blessing, Prosperity, and Longevity Monastery**
4140 Long Beach Boulevard
Long Beach, CA 90807 U.S.A.
Tel: (562) 595-4966


**Avatamsaka Hermitage**
11721 Beall Mountain Road
Potomac, MD 20854-1128 U.S.A.
Tel: (301) 299-3693


**Gold Summit Monastery**
233-1st Ave. West
Seattle, WA 98119 U.S.A.
Tel: (206) 217-9320


**Gold Buddha Monastery**
301 East Hastings Street
Vancouver, BC, V6A 1P3 Canada.
Tel: (604) 684-3754


**Avatamsaka Monastery**
1009-4th Avenue
S.W. Calgary, AB T2P 0K8 Canada.
Tel: (403) 269-2960


**Dharma Realm Buddhist Books Distribution Society**
11th Floor, 85 Chung-hsiao E. Road
Sec. 6, Taipei, R.O.C.
Tel: (02) 786-3022  Fax: (02) 786-2674


**Tze Yun Tung Temple**
Batu 5 1/2, Jalan Sungai Besi, Salak Selatan
57100 Kuala Lumpur, Malaysia
Tel: (03) 782-6560  Fax:(03) 780-1272


**Buddhist Lecture Hall**
31 Wong Nei Chong Road
Top Floor, Happy Valley, Hong Kong
Tel: 2572-7644